100%
UNOFFICIAL

First published in Great Britain 2023 by
100% Unofficial, a part of Farshore

An imprint of HarperCollins*Publishers*
1 London Bridge Street, London SE1 9GF
www.farshore.co.uk

HarperCollins*Publishers*
1st Floor, Watermarque Building, Ringsend Road
Dublin 4, Ireland

Written by Dan Lipscombe
Illustrated and Designed by Matt Burgess

This book is an original creation by Farshore
© 2023 HarperCollinsPublishers Limited

ISBN 978-0-00-861193-4
Printed in Dubai
001

ONLINE SAFETY FOR YOUNGER FANS

Spending time online is great fun! Here are a few simple rules to help younger fans stay safe and
keep the internet a great place to spend time:

- Never give out your real name – don't use it as your username.
- Never give out any of your personal details.
- Never tell anybody which school you go to or how old you are.
- Never tell anybody your password except a parent or a guardian.
- Be aware that you must be 13 or over to create an account on many sites.
Always check the site policy and ask a parent or guardian for permission before registering.
- Always tell a parent or guardian if something is worrying you.

Stay safe online. Any website addresses listed in this book are correct at the time of going to print.
However, Farshore is not responsible for content hosted by third parties. Please be aware that online
content can be subject to change and websites can contain content that is unsuitable for children.
We advise that all children are supervised when using the internet.

Stay safe online. Farshore is not responsible for content hosted by third parties.

100% UNOFFICIAL
FORTNITE
ANNUAL 2024

CONTENTS

WELCOME TO THE WORLD OF FORTNITE!

Everything has been changing in Fortnite since we last saw you – there's been a new chapter, a new map and loads of new stuff to explore! There's never been a better time to drop in!

What do we have for you this year?

We're going to take a look at the recent Fortnite islands, from Chapter 3 all the way through to Chapter 4. To complete the tour we'll seek out some of our favourite Points Of Interest (POIs).

This wouldn't be a Fortnite book without a look at the best in-game weapons and items available to you. We'll help pick the best guns for your play style, but if you're more interested in style, there's a choice selection of skins, harvesters, gliders and back blings.

Once you're fully kitted-out in the right skin, we can travel to some of our favourite creative games or check out a concert in the party world.

Fortnite is still one of the biggest games in the world, with millions of people playing every day. Competitive gamers play for wins, while others just love being in the world of Jones, Peely and Slone. If you're a little confused on the story, we've got a recap of everything that's happened so far.

Now, let's choose our favourite skin and climb aboard the battle bus, ready to fight.

Where we droppin'?

THE MAPS

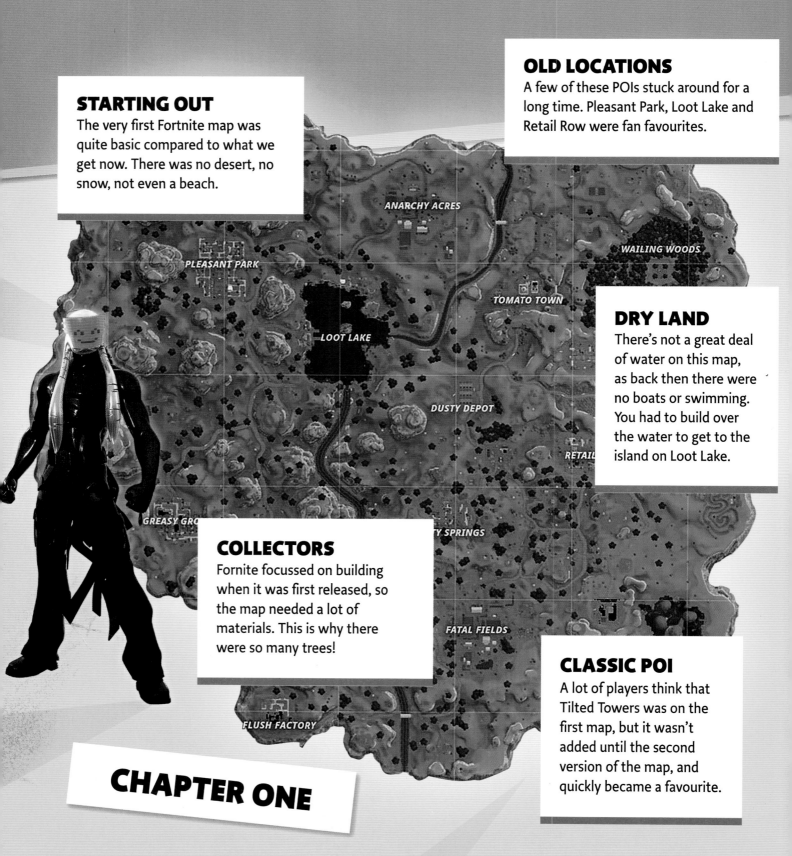

STARTING OUT
The very first Fortnite map was quite basic compared to what we get now. There was no desert, no snow, not even a beach.

OLD LOCATIONS
A few of these POIs stuck around for a long time. Pleasant Park, Loot Lake and Retail Row were fan favourites.

DRY LAND
There's not a great deal of water on this map, as back then there were no boats or swimming. You had to build over the water to get to the island on Loot Lake.

COLLECTORS
Fornite focussed on building when it was first released, so the map needed a lot of materials. This is why there were so many trees!

CLASSIC POI
A lot of players think that Tilted Towers was on the first map, but it wasn't added until the second version of the map, and quickly became a favourite.

ANARCHY ACRES

WAILING WOODS

PLEASANT PARK

TOMATO TOWN

LOOT LAKE

DUSTY DEPOT

RETAIL

GREASY GRO

Y SPRINGS

FATAL FIELDS

FLUSH FACTORY

CHAPTER ONE

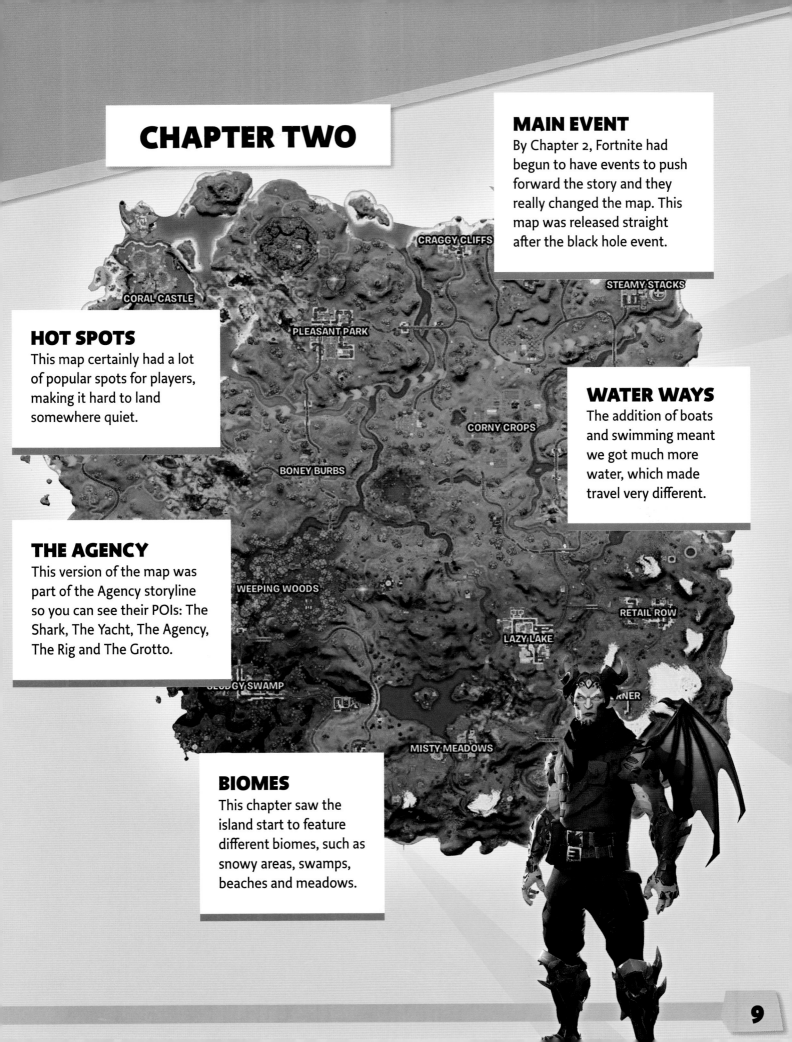

CHAPTER TWO

MAIN EVENT
By Chapter 2, Fortnite had begun to have events to push forward the story and they really changed the map. This map was released straight after the black hole event.

HOT SPOTS
This map certainly had a lot of popular spots for players, making it hard to land somewhere quiet.

WATER WAYS
The addition of boats and swimming meant we got much more water, which made travel very different.

THE AGENCY
This version of the map was part of the Agency storyline so you can see their POIs: The Shark, The Yacht, The Agency, The Rig and The Grotto.

BIOMES
This chapter saw the island start to feature different biomes, such as snowy areas, swamps, beaches and meadows.

The map labels visible:
CORAL CASTLE
CRAGGY CLIFFS
STEAMY STACKS
PLEASANT PARK
CORNY CROPS
BONEY BURBS
WEEPING WOODS
RETAIL ROW
LAZY LAKE
SLURPY SWAMP
MISTY MEADOWS

THE MAPS

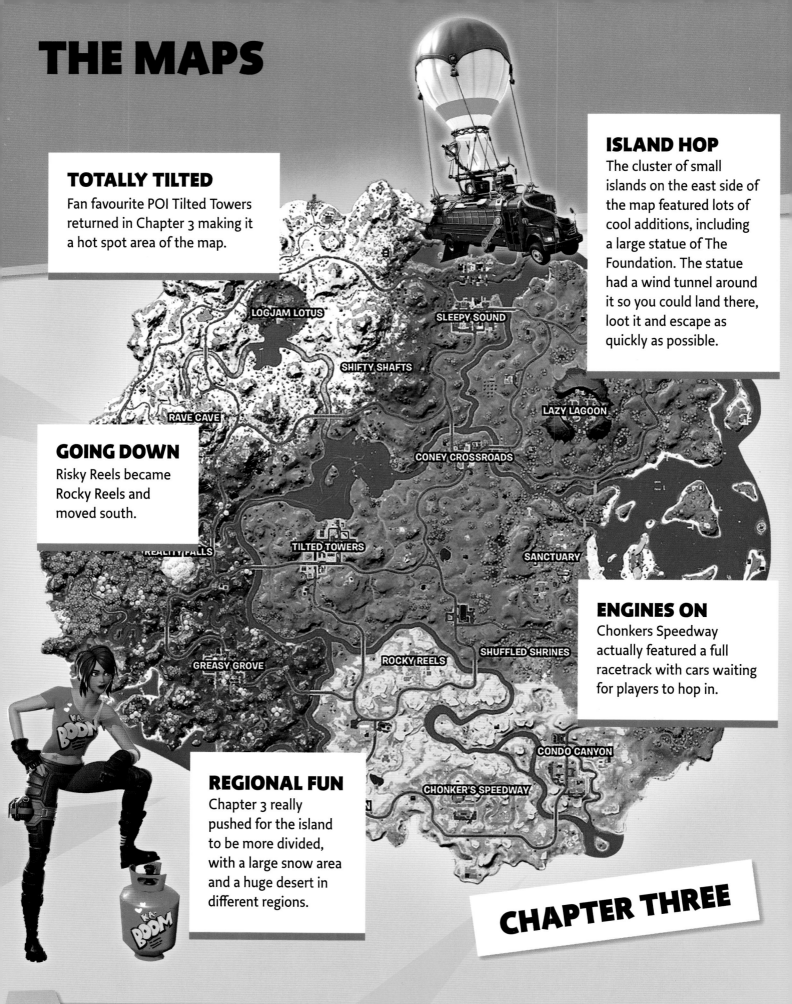

TOTALLY TILTED
Fan favourite POI Tilted Towers returned in Chapter 3 making it a hot spot area of the map.

ISLAND HOP
The cluster of small islands on the east side of the map featured lots of cool additions, including a large statue of The Foundation. The statue had a wind tunnel around it so you could land there, loot it and escape as quickly as possible.

GOING DOWN
Risky Reels became Rocky Reels and moved south.

ENGINES ON
Chonkers Speedway actually featured a full racetrack with cars waiting for players to hop in.

REGIONAL FUN
Chapter 3 really pushed for the island to be more divided, with a large snow area and a huge desert in different regions.

CHAPTER THREE

Map labels:
LOGJAM LOTUS
SLEEPY SOUND
SHIFTY SHAFTS
RAVE CAVE
LAZY LAGOON
CONEY CROSSROADS
REALITY FALLS
TILTED TOWERS
SANCTUARY
GREASY GROVE
ROCKY REELS
SHUFFLED SHRINES
CONDO CANYON
CHONKER'S SPEEDWAY

CHAPTER FOUR

FROSTY FUN
The large snowy area was massive, though it only featured two POIs. If you explored, you could find more buildings like Brutal Bastion, as well as some special snowy secrets.

MIXED UP
Chapter 4 split the map between a modern style and a medieval look. The yellowed areas featured villages and castles, while the forested region had shops and fast food spots.

ON YOUR BIKE
This map introduced dirt bikes which became a fast, and very fun way to travel across the map.

THE CITADEL
The Citadel, the hottest drop on the map, was up in the north west. Normally, these hot drops would sit in the centre.

RIVER RUNS
The map didn't feature a large lake like many of the previous maps. It had a few smaller lakes but rivers still linked the areas together, meaning boats were often your best method of travel.

LONELY LABS

BRUTAL

THE CITADEL

ANVIL SQUARE

FAULTY SPLITS

FRENZY FIELDS

THE POIs

There are always Points of Interest spread across the Fortnite island. Some last for many seasons, while others come and go almost without notice. Here are some highlights!

RETAIL ROW

Retail Row always had a lot of chests and loot, so it proved to be a great place to drop straight from the bus - making it a very hot drop. However, that could sometimes be a bad thing ... when you came up against a strong opponent early on, it was a quick way to end up back in the lobby.

This POI went through some dramatic changes in Chapter 1. In Season 7 two popular spots from Greasy Grove – Durr Burger and Uncle Pete's Pizza Pit – were added. In Season 8, Retail Row was completely destroyed after the volcano erupted in the Nexus Event. Once Season 9 dropped, there wasn't a space for Retail Row, as Mega Mall opened its doors. But due to the popularity of the drop, Season 10 brought Retail Row back from the grave for Fortnitemares.

SWEATY SANDS

Sweaty Sands arrived after the black hole event which opened Chapter 2. It managed to stay in the game for quite a few seasons, although in Season 7 it became Believer Beach – a holiday stop for visiting aliens. A popular spot to land was the high-rise hotel, which contained lots of chests over several floors. Plus, landing there allowed you to hit the ground before others in the area, giving you more time to gather weapons and loot.

There has nearly always been a beach POI in Fortnite, and for a long time it was Sweaty Sands. Named not just because it's hot at the beach, but also because nervous players loved to land at the edges of a map where they felt safer. Sweaty Sands was similar to a fan favourite POI called Paradise Palms, a place you could find ice cream huts, a pier with fishing spots and plenty of bouncy beach umbrellas.

FUN FACT

If you found yourself here, you could search the beach for hidden chests, which could be revealed by smacking the sand with the harvesting tool.

BONEY BURBS

During the Zero Crisis Finale event of Season 6, Chapter 2, fan favurite POI Salty Towers gave way to Boney Burbs.

This small, run-down town almost looks like the ruins of a long forgotten city. Cars submerged in the dirt, old tyres laying around and buildings patched up with torn sheets makes this an easy place to blend in with the surroundings – perfect for stealthy players. With some buildings propped up on stilts, it looks like there was once water surrounding Boney Burbs.

The whole place might look like it needs a lick of paint, but don't let that put you off landing here. There are plenty of buildings and loot chests to be found without being flooded with other players, making it a great drop spot.

IO OUTPOST

Over time, Fortnite players noticed these outposts popping up across the island. They were put there by the Imagined Order, who built them on top of the huge holes created by the Mole Teams.

While they were all small in size, they contained high tech instruments and security to keep the Imagined Order's secrets safe. Of course there was loot to be had, too – but not enough to make them a super popular drop zone. This made them relatively safe in the early stages of every battle but a dangerous place to hide if they were in the centre of the final storm circle.

THE POIs

PLEASANT PARK

Ahhh, Pleasant Park. This POI is one of the most important in Fortnite history as it was one of the first locations when the game launched. It had been around since Season 1 and right up through to Chapter 2. When Pleasant Park was removed with Chapter 3, it was the first time the game hadn't featured this classic POI.

Pleasant Park has been home to an evil genius, who had an underground base which split the football field in half. In the Primal season it was even completely blocked off. Along with Tilted Towers, this POI was popular due to the number of chests and places to fight. It was filled with small houses for cramped battles and the larger park area was perfect for building or long-range shots.

Many players who would drop here did so because loot chests often spawned in attics. This made the houses seriously tempting. As you would glide into the area, you could look around and see everyone else doing the same thing. Everyone touched down on the roof, hacked away with their pickaxe and grabbed loot before they could be attacked. What a rush!

ANVIL SQUARE

Found near the centre of the island, Anvil Square is considered by many players to be an all-time classic POI. Landing there is like being transported to a medieval time, with old fashioned buildings and towers standing tall over the town.

Due to its location and abundance of loot, landing here at the start of a match is only advised for experienced players. There will be lots of competition early on ... but don't worry about missing out. Survive long enough and there's a good chance the storm circle will close in here. If it does, this will give you the opportunuity to explore and battle your way through its maze of buildings and yards - just make sure your loadout and health is as full as possible!

CORNY CROPS

This classic area of farmland has taken on many different appearances over the years. Before Corny Crops, it was known as Corny Complex – a POI that might have looked like a few harmless barns, but it was packed with secret high tech machinery.

As Corny Crops, it will come as no surprise that there are many corn fields in and around the location, making it a great place for taking cover. There are also foragable items with unexpected benefits, such as cabbage. This leafy little consumable might not look like much, but it will slowly heal up to 10 health points. Because buildings are few and far between, they will be hot property for anyone dropping in – so act fast or consider looting in a different location at the start of every new battle.

THE POIs

THE CITADEL

The medieval centre, called The Citadel, is one of the more recent POIs on this list. Appearing in the first season of Chapter 4, this vast castle was perched on top of a hill. A watery moat circled the hill, making it difficult to get in or out without bumping into other players. The castle was home to The Ageless, a new character to Fortnite who dressed in white and gold armour and carried a sword that shot energy charges.

Inside the castle, players could find a new chest called the Oathbound chest. These larger, white and gold chests would drop more weapons and items. The Oathbound chest would often contain the Shockwave Hammer which could smash players with supreme force and catapult them across the map.

BELIEVER BEACH

Why not put on your swimming costume, get some ice cream and enjoy the cool ocean? We'll tell you why not – because there's a battle raging and this is no time for a holiday!

Believer Beach looked exactly like Sweaty Sands, the resort which previously stood in its position. Most of the buildings were the same and chilling on the beach was just as tempting, apart from the mysterious alien markings drawn into the sand.

There were also several environmental crash pads found only here. These mad contraptions could be thrown to unleash a gravity-defying trampoline to take off from!

HOLLY HEDGES

With a name like Holly Hedges, it should come as no surprise that there is a gardening theme to this massively popular POI. It's easy to identify as you glide high over the island, thanks to the open grassland, pristine hedges and the rolling hills that surround the town and lead directly to the island's edge.

Once you decide this is where you're going to drop, it's a matter of choosing where your first steps should be. There are only a few buildings to pick and most of them are standard housing structures – but these do contain multiple looting options, and usually several chests. Because of this, there is always strong competition in the early stages of every battle. Landing here makes the first minutes of each battle incredibly rushed.

To avoid the crowded and potentially deadly houses, many players opt to choose different landing spots in the land surrounding Holly Hedges. If you land closer to the sea, there are several warehouse style structures that make for some awesome open-air battles and looting opportunites, but there's also a higher risk of needed to rush away from the storm circle when closes in.

It might be one of the smallest named locations on the island, but there are plenty of reasons that it's one of the most popular. If the coast is clear and you have time, why not check out the local garden centre? It's full of places to hide and, err, lots of lovely garden gnomes. Just don't mistake them for opponents!

THE POIs

FUN FACT!

The end of Chapter 2, Season 7, saw all the Slurp Juice cleared out and the swamp became an ordinary swamp, renamed as Sludgy Swamp.

SLURPY SWAMP

Slurp Juice is a big part of Fortnite. If it wasn't for this odd blue liquid, we wouldn't have shields while fighting. After the black hole closed and Chapter 2 began, we found a factory for Slurp Juice on the map. The factory was huge, with lots of different sized rooms for fighting and exploring.

Perhaps its best feature was the swamp outside, which was being polluted with Slurp Juice. This made the water around the POI a healing body of water. You knew that if you landed there you could get to full shield within a short period of time. Or, if you got into an early fight, a quick dash through Slurpy Swamp would heal you nicely. Nowadays you're likely to find Slap Juice, as well as Slurpy!

DIRTY DOCKS

Dirty Docks was always a fun place to drop into. It often contained an NPC character selling great weapons, and it also housed lots of chests. There were often boats sat at the water's edge for a quick getaway either north or south. The Docks were a place you could land quickly due to the height of the crane that contained a chest. Players would often land on the chest here, before dropping down to explore elsewhere.

Oddly, the Docks were another place to find a small football field. It was tucked near the back, next to the largest warehouse. Dirty Docks, much like others on this list, has been removed. We saw the POI disappear during The End event in Season 8 of Chapter 2 and it hasn't returned since.

STEAMY STACKS

An all-time classic POI. Steamy Stacks felt like it was always on the island, but it was only introduced at the start of Chapter 2, Season 1. Since then it survived several story-related events, such as severe flooding, a spaceship, and severely influenced by the Imagined Order.

It was one of the easiest POIs to recognise as soon as players jumped out of the Battle Bus, making it a popular dropspot. Thanks to its secret underground bunkers, there was lots of loot to be had and lots of cover in the early stages of the battle.

Sadly, Steamy Stacks suffered a sad fate when it found itself underneath the island's surface and was then destroyed by the Chrome. It was last spotted when a tower was seen floating through space!

LONELY LABS

Another more recent POI, Lonely Labs is a nightmare to fight in, but also the most fun. As an arctic research centre, it's built on ice and snow. The buildings are filled with tiny rooms where a shotgun blast is likely to eliminate you outright, and the ground outside cannot be trusted. Just stepping foot on the ice here is a risk as you slide all over the place, making it hard to aim your weapons with any accuracy.

The labs feature lots of secret space underneath where you can either hide away, or catch opponents unaware. While it isn't the most interesting looking POI, you can guarantee that an ending circle here is going to be pure carnage.

FUN FACT!

Lonely Labs is one of the smallest POIs ever. It's also sat on top of an iceberg.

THE SKINS:
BEST OF THE BATTLE PASS

Unlocking one of your favourite skins is an exciting achievement and can help you keep playing as them long after they leave the Fortnite store. Here are our faves!

MEOWSCLES

One of the big fan favourites from The Agency of Chapter 2, was Meowscles. This buff kitty cat was known as the muscle for Midas' gang. Found down in Catty Corner, Meowscles set himself up a little home in the gas station, complete with a litter box and cat tower. It was hard to believe he was one of the bad guys considering how cute he was.

Players unlocking Meowscles had a tricky decision to make, becasue you had to side with either Ghost or Shadow, which would change the look of the skin. This couldn't be switched after the choice was made, but both looked great. Either the black and grey Shadow look, or white and gold for Ghost.

If you played this season, which did you choose?

GUMBO

A random food object becomes a fighter in the Fortnite universe, with Gumbo appearing in Chapter 3, Season 1. You can probably tell what food has been transformed here. Gumbo's head is one enormous gumball and his outfit leans into the bright colours that we think of with this candy.

If you look closely, his headphones are squished and melted gumballs stuck to his head, so he must love enjoying his music, or maybe a podcast, while he's exploring the battlefield. As part of the 'Chew It Yourself' set, he came with a large gumball glider with the derpiest face ever and big bug eyes.

MANCAKE

Fortnite loves to offer skins which turn animals or objects into a person. Mancake is the perfect example. How does a stack of yummy pancakes become a person with weapons? As you can see, Mancake is completed by sticky syrup over his head, with a cube of butter melting in his hand. In fact, around his neck, instead of ammo, he has bars of butter!

Mancake could be found in the desert area of the map, playing as a cowboy. We're not sure how successful he would be as a cowboy as everything would stick to him. Perhaps he makes people slip on butter before robbing them, or whipping out his pistols to eliminate them!

HELSIE

One of the more recent skins is this Boba Tea-obsessed fighter called Helsie. Helsie has two jobs; by day she works as a Boba Tea barista, while at night she hunts vampires. Quite a difference between the two, right? Helsie is always up for a brawl, as long as she can stop for Boba. In fact, she has an emote which involves riding a cluster of Boba balls as it wriggles across the ground.

Helsie has a unique style of her own. She can keep you safe from blood-drinking monsters and can make you an epic drink, too. She's quirky and dangerous, which is a deadly combination. Thank goodness she's on our side of the fight!

THE BEST OF THE GUNS

Fortnite often changes up its loot every time a new season drops, and even throughout a season, we will see new weapons come and go.

TOP TIP!

After that first shot, be prepared for this weapon to do less damage and fire slowly. It stays true though, so the lack of damage per second (DPS) is made up for with accuracy.

HEAVY ASSAULT RIFLE

The heavy assault rifle is a slow-firing weapon where that important first bullet can really wreck an enemy's shield. Landing that first shot will pack so much damage that the slow rate of fire doesn't matter. You can pair this AR with a more rapid-fire weapon, switching to this after you've fired the first bullet.

DRUM GUN

The drum gun mixes together assault rifles and SMGs. A really-rapid firing weapon that has good range. Although this gun doesn't have a high damage stat, due to the number of shots it will fire, the damage per second (DPS) is great!

MK-SEVEN ASSAULT RIFLE

You may find more accuracy from this newer style of assault rifle. In Chapter 3, Fortnite introduced guns that would put you into first-person view when aiming. This means you see through your characters eyes. This style of aiming can help when trying to pin down an opponent.

BURST ASSAULT RIFLE

If you're after a long range rifle that has great accuracy, then a burst rifle is best. It has the power of other rifles, but you won't waste as much ammo from missed shots. The burst rifle tends to hit hard due to the first shot mechanic in Fortnite, where the first bullet is the most accurate and damaging.

TOP TIP!

You can still hold the trigger down to keep firing, but your shots will be all over the place. Tap firing is key here.

TOP TIP!

A great gun for early in the game. Finding this in your first chest is a bonus because it'll hurt those who dropped around you. Once you have a decent AR though, drop this right away.

HAND CANNON

It's safe to say that most of the pistols in Fortnite get left behind. Why would you use one when there are more reliable and higher damage weapons? The hand cannon, however, is a great choice if you can land your shots. This weapon packs such a punch that opponents won't know what hit them until the stat screen appears!

EX-CALIBER RIFLE

This rifle came with Chapter 4's first season. It's a gun that fires energy swords at people, which is bonkers! It's not a great rifle, but it gets included here because it's so different. To be fair, it does have decent damage, but other rifles will outperform it due to its fire-rate.

AUTO SHOTGUN

All of the shotguns can really hurt opposing players. The auto shotgun has a low damage profile compared to others, but it fires so quickly it won't even matter. This is a perfect close-combat weapon for when the other player is jumping around, as you can hold the trigger and try to follow their movements.

TOP TIP!

Take an extra second to line up that shot and use this as a short-range sniper. When the swords hit, they hurt, but spraying this gun makes it useless.

DMR

If you struggle with the timing when using a sniper rifle and you're missing your target, a DMR might be better. The DMR doesn't feature the high damage of a sniper, but it's a semi-auto, which means you can keep tapping the trigger and fire rapidly. This will pepper your enemy with several shots, rather than rely on one big hit.

TOP TIP!

A brilliant gun for keeping an enemy pinned down inside a building. Due to its fast firing, you can pop off shots whenever someone pokes their head outside and they'll dash back in. Send a friend around the back to finish them off while you sit at range.

THE BEST OF THE GUNS

TOP TIP!

Not just a weapon, the shockwave hammer can smash into the ground and catapult you across the landscape. It's awesome for moving around quickly.

SHOCKWAVE HAMMER

The shockwave hammer is a nasty weapon when you get hit by it, but the timing to hit an opponent is tricky to master. Because this weapon needs to be slightly charged before it hits, you need to read where your enemy might move to. Then, you can be ready to whack them.

TOP TIP!

Try not to use this up close, it'll still hit hard, but it's a fair bit harder to aim when someone is right in front of you.

COMBAT SHOTGUN

This variant of the shotgun is perfect for a range of combat styles. It provides a hard hit, but holds much less ammo. This is because it's better used with a bit more space between you and your target. This is a ranged weapon and, due to that, the damage carries better through the air with a more clustered shot.

QUAD LAUNCHER

This lean, mean lobbing machine was capable of launching four rockets in quick succession, causing unthinkable damage to other players and their structures. It was vaulted due to being immensely overpowered – but Fortnite players will always remember it, for it's unique powers of fear and destruction.

PUMP SHOTGUN

The most popular shotgun in the game, for many reasons, but mostly because of its high damage. You need to be a bit more accurate as this shotgun fires slowly and takes a while to reload. If you're missing your shots, it's likely you will end up back in the lobby pretty quickly.

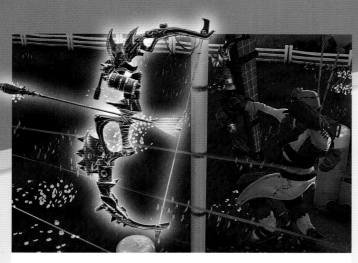

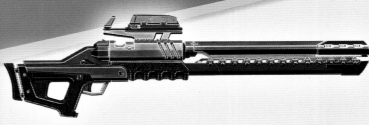

PRIMAL FLAME BOW

This is a great weapon against builders, as it can set fire to a wooden build quickly. Outside of that, you can use it to clear trees which might be in the way of your shots, or just to keep your opponent pinned down. Fire makes most players panic, so it can be used tactically to terrific effect.

RAIL GUN

The only true 'hit-scan' weapon in Fortnite. The rail gun releases a beam while it charges up the shot. This means you can track the enemy from quite far away and land that mad shot. It's perfect for taking out vehicles, but can be used on players as well, as long as you know where they will be by the time the charging finishes.

TOP TIP!

Follow your target with the beam, but get used to how long it takes to fire. Once you have that timing down, you'll be a crack shot. This is also great against any build material.

HEAVY SNIPER RIFLE

The nastiest sniper rifle in Fortnite is here! It's so nasty that it fires incredibly slowly. You have to reload after every shot, which can take up time. If you aren't accurate, you can find yourself spotted after you've fired it and the enemy will have time to fire back. If you do hit a headshot though, they're back in the lobby.

TOP TIP!

This is such a slow weapon, but it's great for eliminating any downed opponents, especially from far away. Your teammate can knock someone and move on, knowing you'll finish off the job.

ROCKET LAUNCHER

Most people don't use the rocket launcher to actually eliminate people but it's more of a fun weapon. It can cause some carnage, or drop a building, it's unlikely to knock down anyone unless they have no shields. Even then, there's a high chance you take yourself out, unless you've fired it from a distance.

THE BEST OF THE GUNS

COMPACT SMG

Many players prefer an SMG to a shotgun because they can track enemy movements with it and pepper them with shots. You don't have to be as accurate with an SMG, as so many bullets will be fired. It does require a lot of reloading though, so it becomes a balance. The compact is a heavy hitter and is often vaulted due to how deadly it can be.

TOP TIP!

It's possible to shoot this at your friends and heal them while they're facing off against another player. It's the splash that coats them in the slurp, so you don't need to be accurate.

CHUG CANNON

Can a chug cannon be a weapon? It is a gun, after all. Though this gun does no damage, it's used to heal yourself or your team. Just fire a blast of bright blue slurp at your feet to top-up your shields. You can play the medic on your team by carrying this and firing it at your friends in the middle of a brutal battle to keep them in the match longer!

LIGHT MACHINE GUN

The light machine gun sits between AR and SMG. It fires incredibly quickly for such a big gun. The damage is neither amazing or rubbish. It sits in the middle, but holding the trigger button unleashes a stream of shots that will force other players to take cover. It's a great weapon for holding others at bay while your team surrounds them or takes cover.

TOP TIP!

A big magazine means this weapon doesn't need reloading as often, which is great because it takes ages.

FLINT-KNOCK PISTOL

The flint-knock isn't a very good weapon in a fight and you'd choose so many more guns before this one. However, this pistol can help you move around the map much faster. Firing it in the opposite direction you want to move, will blast you forwards. It's great for launching into a POI to take unsuspecting players by surprise!

HOP ROCK DUALIES

There aren't many weapons that alter how your character moves but the hop rock dualies do just this. Equipping them activates low gravity for you, meaning you can jump much higher, which will fool those around you. This does mean you'll jump slower as well, so it can make you a bit of a target.

TOP TIP!

If you're fast enough, you can use the low-gravity jump going upwards, then switch to another gun at the top of the jump for one on the way back down.

PRIMAL PISTOL

This unique weapon fires in small bursts of two shots, providing a little more firepower than the standard pistols. While it can deal large doses of damage, it suffers in the accuracy department and can leave you flailing in long-range shootouts.

TOP TIP!

If you find yourself face to face with someone just after dropping, this SMG can quickly send them back to the lobby. It's great straight after landing, but other guns will shine as you keep looting.

BOOM BOW

Making things go boom is a lot of fun in Fortnite. The boom bow, which first appeared with The Agency, can turn any build into rubble. It can blast enemies from their high ground hiding places. It can cause carnage, completely distracting enemies while you run at them.

RAPID FIRE SMG

If you thought an SMG couldn't fire any faster, then think again! The rapid fire SMG lacks a lot of hard damage, but it can overwhelm an opponent completely as they struggle to escape a hail storm of shots. It's perfect for inside buildings or small rooms, as your opponent will have nowhere to run to.

GETTING CREATIVE 1

One of the secret skills of a super Fortnite player is the ability to build in Creative mode. Not sure where to start? You can be inspired by and play islands created by other players!

ENTER A VALID ISLAND CODE BELOW:

0123-4567-8910

Enter an **Island Code** to load a creator's island.

HOW TO USE ISLAND CODES?

- Open the game mode screen.
- Scroll along the options at the very top. Go past Discover, Browse, My Library and Create. You want the Island Code option.
- Simply head into this tab and type in the code you want to use.
- If you fancy making your own islands, just jump into the Create tab instead!

PROP HUNT 3948-7015-9316

Prop Hunt has been around for so long, it feels like we've been playing it for years. Some players are yet to try out this classic game though.
If you've never tried it, the rules are simple, it's basically hide and seek. Players are separated into hiders and seekers. The seekers have access to weapons and must find and eliminate the hiders.

The hiders though, have a prop gun. Aim this gun at any object or item in the world and you will become a double of it. So, fire it at a teddy bear and you become a teddy bear. Then you can hide and try to blend in with the others. Be careful though, any movement will give away your position!

PRISON BREAK 0893-8977-9494

A classic escape map, Prison Break asks you if you want to escape or catch criminals. It's your choice and both offer a lot of fun. The map supports 24 players and features quests as well as difficult parkour challenges. If you choose to break out, you'll need to dodge the guards and work with other prisoners to see success.

If you want to eliminate players who are escaping, you can choose the role of guard and chase them down, shoot at them, or tease them into making a mistake. It's up to you to stop the Prison Break!

THE MAZE RUNNER 7365-7356-7149

Mazes can either be brilliant or horrible. This one is huge and rather brilliant, as long as you have tips for finding your way back out. Maps like this can be entertaining as just a simple maze; you can play by yourself or work with your friends to see if you can escape and complete the challenges together.

Why not form teams and try to see who can eliminate the most zombies? Or see who can survive in the maze at night for the longest time? Remember to gather crafting materials, and craft some good weapons, or you'll struggle – these maze zombies pack a punch! Or you can just chill and enjoy the central zone, hiding and playing in there.

THE ITEMS

Fortnite isn't only about weapons – mastering the use of items is a game changer. They can be used for healing, accessing weapons or disturbing opponents. Over the years Fortnite has been with us plenty of items have come and gone – which are your favourites?

CREEPIN' CARDBOARD

We'd say it's highly unlikely that opposing players will stop to inspect every box they see on the island, which is why this was such a useful tool. You could put this item on and still walk, sprint and build as much as you wanted to – and then hide at a moment's notice. This was so useful for catching unsuspecting players with surprise attacks!

MEAT

Animal cruelty ahead! If you're really desperate for health ... we mean REALLY desperate ... you could shoot down a crow or chicken, maybe even a boar or wolf. This will leave you with some meat that can be munched and restore 15 health. Meat isn't as good as basic meds for healing chunks of health points, but you can eat it while moving, which beats bandages that need you to stand still.

SMALL SHIELD POTION

These are often called 'minis' by most players because they're the smallest bottles. They give the player 25 shield points but can only be used until you have 50 shield points. Once you've hit 50, you need to use a 'big pot'. This is the most basic item in Fortnite, but it's probably the most important!

SHIELD KEG

A newer way to apply shields is the shield keg. At first, the kegs could be hard to find, but nowadays they spawn pretty regularly. This healing item is brilliant during team play, as it applies shields to everyone at the same time. To use the keg, you simply throw it on the ground and it sprays shield potion in a tight circle. If everyone gathers around, you can all get to 100 shield super fast.

RIFT-TO-GO

Need to escape a situation fast? Pop a Rift-To-Go and you can redeploy from a rift in the sky. In fact, so can your whole team if you're standing close together. Be careful though, if the enemy is close, they can either be caught in your rift, or rush the rift point on the ground and follow you through the air!

PIZZA PARTY

This rare item can be used to deliver eight slices of pizza in one throw. A slice of pizza can restore both 25 health and 25 shield points, making it a delicious boost during any battle. A pizza party is a superb item for any team modes, as it can fuel your whole squad. Just be prepared – you may survive longer but there isn't a dip in sight!

MED MIST

A full heal can feel so good when you've had a horrible fight that has left you on 5hp, or you've trudged through the storm and are close to death. Back in the day you'd have to hunker down and spend time using a medkit. With the med mist you can keep moving, and even use it while sliding. You can even spray your mates and get them healed up. A-tier healing right here!

ZERO POINT CRYSTALS

These crystals pop up every now and again and they are guaranteed to cause a bit of chaos. They allow the player to teleport a short distance in the direction they're facing. Blink and you'll miss it! It's a great item for keeping your enemy guessing as you can approach them from one direction, start a fight, then teleport behind them to finish.

BANDAGES

Healing 15 health points doesn't sound like much, but you can use bandages up to 75 health. While it's always best to carry full medkits, bandages while on the go can save your game. These can be used more quickly than a medkit, so if you've got enemies on you, they will get you fighting faster.

THE ITEMS

SKY JELLIES

So cute and so helpful, sky jellies will grant you health or shields while bouncing you high in the air. These are very similar to the mushrooms found in Chapter 3, which did the same thing. Jellies move in groups though, so you can hang around and bounce off several in order to fully-heal up before moving on.

MUSHROOM

Mushrooms grow in patches in the heavily wooded areas and can often be missed by players in a rush. They are a lifesaver in bad times. If you're struggling to find shields and stumble across a scattering of the blue mushrooms, these can get you back in the fight. They only give 5 shield points, but they can help in a pinch.

JUNK RIFT

Junk rifts never seem to do much damage to players, but they're brilliant and fun to use. Watching on as furniture, structures and junk rain down from a rift in the sky is always funny. And if you manage to smash a player in the head, then it's a bonus. If using it for damage doesn't help you, you can call in all that junk nearby and use it to harvest materials instead.

HOT SPOTS

A strange name for these drones, but they mark out an area which will be a hot drop or a popular area. Inside the cargo pod on these drones will be a rare or better weapon. It's ideal to land here, grab a rubbish grey pistol and blast down a drone. You could end up leaving the area with a rare purple weapon to engage in fun fights faster.

AIR STRIKE

This is a much better item for raining damage onto opponents from the sky. The air strike fires several missiles from above, causing plenty of damage to either players or builds. It's a great item to bring down a building where your opponent may be hiding, or you can use it to stop them from moving on to pin them down in a location.

SLAP JUICE

Better than a slap in the face, Slap Juice will regenerate lost energy for 50 seconds. What's more, it will make your feet glow orange while it's operation – pretty cool. If you throw one, it will send a ping once it lands, alerting your squad to its location. You can stack up to six at any time, and use it while moving, making it a must-grab item if you see any while looting!

GUZZLE JUICE

The Guzzle Juice doesn't come back to Battle Royale very often, but it's a lovely healing item when it does. This heals over time, so it's great to drink it down before charging across the map or running through the storm. It will slowly increase your health while you move, loot or shoot. Saving a lot of time can be super helpful, especially if you're having a good game.

SHIELD BUBBLE

The shield bubble is great for quickly protecting you or your team from getting shot at. It spawns an instant bubble around you which stops shots from getting through. It doesn't stop an opponent from rushing you and bringing the fight close, though. They can be thrown down behind you as you run away to protect your backs.

CHUG SPLASH

One of the most popular consumable healing items, the chug splash made a real ... er, splash, when it was first found on the island. If you throw it within a splash radius of your team, everyone will be 20 health points better off. It can be found all across the island in a variety of locations, but it is rare – so if you do see any, make sure to pick them up!

GONE FISHING

Fishing appeared in Fortnite Chapter 2, when the water first became something we could swim in, and travel across. For a long while, all we could catch were floppers and slurpfish, which were definitely helpful, but there wasn't much variety. Nowadays there are lots of fish to catch and they even come in different colours!

SLURPFISH

Much like the jellyfish, a slurpfish heals either health or shields, depending on your need. But, this fish restores 40 health points – double the strength of the jellyfish! They are harder to find, though, so check out the fish freezers in POIs for a chance to find them.

SMALL FRY

The most basic fish you can catch will heal 25 health, up to 75. They offer the same benefits as bandages, but small fry fish offer much faster healing.

FLOPPER

Floppers heal 40 health points, but are consumed much faster than any other healing item. You can carry a few of these and they will heal you back to full health in seconds.

JELLYFISH

Jellyfish will heal 20 health points or shields, depending on what you need the most. As with all other fish here, it's used super-fast and can save the day in a pinch.

SPICY FISH

The spicy fish heals 15 points, but it super-charges your movement speed. Now you can dash about to your heart's content.

ZERO POINT FLOPPER

Heals for 15 points of health, but also allows you to teleport around for a short period of time. This is another hard-to-find fish, but it's great to find one and start teleporting around the map.

HOP FLOPPER

Hop Flopper's provide 15 health points, but also the popular low-gravity jump. Munch this and save yourself from horrible fall damage.

RIFT FISH

A brilliant fish to chomp with mates around. This fish heals 15 points of health, but also creates a rift and drops you and your team from the sky to regroup. Its epic rarity makes it really hard to find!

MIDAS FLOPPER

A strange legendary fish that is rarely seen; the Midas flopper will heal for 40 points, but even better, it will turn every weapon you have into legendary versions. This completely changes your game, as now your weapons are more powerful.

CUDDLE FISH

The cuddle fish is quite rare to find. When thrown at enemies it can stick to them and cause damage. Don't worry if you miss your throw though – it will still cause damage when the enemy walks nearby.

SHADOW FLOPPER

This fish doesn't heal you, but it will make you feel powerful. Eating a shadow flopper turns you into a shadow, which will speed you up, but also make you indestructible for a short time. This is great for escaping a difficult fight!

VENDETTA FLOPPER

As a legendary fish, the vendetta flopper is difficult to catch. Healing for 40 points of health, it's as powerful as the standard flopper, but this one will also highlight a nearby enemy for you to hunt down.

STINK FLOPPER

The poor stink flopper looks so miserable, but you would be too if you smelled this bad! This fish can be eaten for 20 health, or you can throw it at an enemy to cause a stinky cloud of damaging gas.

SNOWY FLOPPER

It might be harder to control your player when their feet are frozen, but they certainly move a lot faster. It can help get you from point A to point B, so munching a snowy flopper will freeze your feet and give you 40 points of health.

THERMAL FISH

Another legendary fish, the thermal fish heals for 40 points, but it also changes your vision. Now you can see other players highlighted as warm red outlines, while the landscape appears in cooler colours. It's great for spotting enemies hiding in buildings.

THE SKINS

Fortnite skins are the main way to express yourself when playing. Everyone has their favourite skins but some people use a different one for each match. There are so many amazing designs to choose from, and some players love collecting them. We've explored every skin to bring you the very best of the best. Take a look at these legends!

ORO

Oro is a blinged-out skeleton with an epic glowing crown. Are its bones covered in gold, or is it made of solid gold shaped into bones? Maybe they had a fight with Midas. Whatever the answer, they look so cool. Their clothes have an almost tattered look to them, which could be a result of living underground - but is likely down to being in so many battle royales.

This isn't the best skin for hiding in bushes as the gold will really make you stand out. But at least you'll look good while playing.

DJ BOP

DJ Bop looks like Cuddle Team Leader got trapped in a disco. She's such a bright colour. With her floaty skirt and disco ball top, she's going to turn heads while cranking 90 tunes at her deck. DJ Bop is the perfect skin for busting out dancing emotes. With a few Boogie Bombs, she will watch you dance before eliminating you with a quick shotgun blast.

DJ Bop is an ideal skin to use during the Fortnite concerts because she really looks the part. Which back bling would you use with these eye-popping colours?

GALAXIA

The legendary Galaxia was the first outfit ever unlockable by being part of the Fortnite Crew. They are based on the classic original skin, Ramirez, but have a much more exciting, space-age appearance, similar to the Galaxy Scout outfit.

While their outfit suggests they have the power to destroy entire planets, we can't confirm this ability. All we know for sure is that in your hands, this outfit is capable of winning any battle ... just as long as those glowing gold eyes don't stand out to enemies too much!

SNAP

Snap may be part of the Spare Parts set, but we think this look is too cool to only be a spare part. If you used your Battle Stars to unlock it, you were given Snap quests – complete these and you gained the ability to customize the skin.

Players could change different elements of the skin by removing and adding body parts. This might sound a bit messy but the result was a new skin that was totally unique to you!

THE SKINS

AXO

This cute little lizard is no stranger to challenges. After all, it came from the sea and adapted to dry land so it could compete in battle royales. Its signature style is a basketball-loving humanoid, but its variant style of midnight colours and neon green details really stands out at night.

Axo also has some epic accessories, with an Axe-olotl harvesting tool and Neon Backboard basketball back bling! We'd love to shoot hoops – and some enemies – with this legend.

MASSAI

Fortnite outfits don't come much cooler than Massai ... unless you consider its variant styles, that is. Air Walker Massai and Thrasher Massai both come with awesome masks that add an element of mystery to any battlefield. Nothing strikes more fear into your opponents than a mask!

Whichever variant you play as, their accessories are just as cool. With a Flip Flyer glider and Board Breaker harvesting tool, you'll look like a boss at all times.

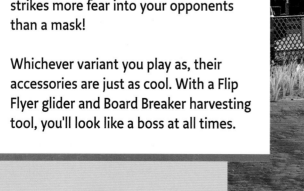

LEELAH

If you're ready to hit the slopes and survive in the snowy areas, without losing your sense of style, then LeeLah is the skin for you. We've never seen socks look as warm as those, even if they leave your legs a bit cold. This outfit is perfect for the winter months, when surviving the conditions is as important as surving the battle.

LeeLah's back bling, Hoppabuns, could be the cutest on the island, considering it comes in the Best Friends bundle, but its arms reaching for a cuddle could be a bit sinister!

DOMINION

Dominion is not here to mess around. This demonic devil only cares about causing carnage and eliminating everyone he meets. He's not very scary, compared to a lot of other skins. In fact, he actually looks awesome. With the fashionable ripped trousers, the fire pattern on his skin and the chains he's using as jewellery, he looks pretty stylish.

We'd rather he was on our side of the fight. Nobody wants to battle a demon, surely?! And is that shotgun ammo on his belt? Maybe Dominion likes to drop shot his enemies.

THE LANGUAGE

Fortnite has spawned so many new phrases and sayings that players pick up from playing together, or watching content creators. Over the years some have come and gone, while others stick around forever.
Which of these do you know? And which have you used while playing?

"CRACKED"

When someone is truly great at the game, they're cracked.

"OP"

OP stands for OverPowered. This normally sums up a weapon that seems to eliminate people quickly or has high damage.

"CRANKING 90s"

For traditional Fortnite with building, '90s' is a form of building quickly. It involves laying a floor, ramp, then turning 90 degrees to place another floor and ramp. This is a quick way of gaining height in a build-fight.

"ROTATE"

Rotating is what happens when a player moves around the map as the storm approaches. A rotation will usually pass through a set route that the player is used to and can provide extra loot.

"DUB"

A 'dub' comes from shortening the word for 'W', which stands for a win. The opposite of this would be an 'L' standing for loss.

"FULL SEND"

To full send is to run-up on an opponents aggressively, all guns blazing. This can happen as a team or on your own.

"FLEX"

Flexing on someone happens when you've eliminated a player and immediately use a dance emote. It's a cheeky way to show off.

"THIRSTING"

If you've knocked a player and immediately run up on them to finish them off, you're thirsty for the elimination. Thirsting usually happens when you want to reduce a team by a player so they can't attack at full strength.

"SWEAT"

Sometimes you'll meet players that just seem to push every fight with so many good guns in their inventory. These are usually people who play the game non-stop and they're called sweats.

"LASER BEAM"

When someone manages to drop your health rapidly, particularly from far away, it's like being hit by a laser beam.

"HOT DROP"

Hot dropping means jumping out of the battle bus early or at a very popular POI (Point of Interest) like Tilted Towers. These usually result in early fights.

"BLUE 55"

Calling out 'blue' is a way of telling everyone you've hit someone's shield. The number is what pops up on the screen. For example, "Blue 55" means you taken 55 points off their shield, leaving 45 behind.

"KNOCKED!"

If you damage a player enough in a team game they will fall to the floor, waiting for someone to revive them. This is when they're knocked, meaning 'knocked to the floor'.

"ONE TAP"

This is a one shot elimination, usually from a sniper rifle headshot.

"THEY'RE FLESH!"

This is a team callout for when you've broken an opponent's shield leaving them on basic health.

THE HARVESTERS

Whether you play Build or No Build, your character always has their trusty harvesting tool. What started out as a pickaxe has become something else over time. You can still find pickaxes, but there's also dual axes, long poles and weirdly shaped hammers. Choosing your favourite harvester is just as important as choosing some of the best skins.

ASTRAL AXE

Swing through the stars with this Season 8 harvesting tool. Found in the Interstellar set, the Astral Axe was used by the terrifying Luminos and was so epic that it almost took the attention away from its metallic and birdlike helmet.

BITEMARK

Bitemark isn't the scariest-looking dinosaur we've ever seen, which makes sense when you realise it was part of the Dino Guard set. The Slurp-o-saurus Rex skin was just a humanoid dressed as a dinosaur, which made them look more like they were going to a fancy dress party than a battle royale!

EPIC SWORDS OF WONDER

Any weapons or harvesting tools you can dual-wield always look instantly cool, and the Epic Swords of Wonder are no exception. You can sheath them in the back bling, in the Adventure Pack, and you'll instantly look like you're ready for any adventure your opponents can throw at you. Wonderful!

CHAINSAUR

Would you look at that? Just when you thought you'd seen the scariest harvesting tools available, they bring you this. Straight from the Bone Punk set, this roarsome piece of kit is the definition of a bone saw! Those razor sharp chainsaw teeth won't harvest materials any quicker than other tools, but they will look meaner – especially coupled with the Bone Patrol glider!

ANARCHY AXE

Nothing will start a battle royale rebellion as ferociously as the Anarchy Axe. As part of the Volume 11 set, it is the loudest harvester on the island – especially when it's being used by Power Chord or Riot outfits. Those punks love a good battle party!

LLAMINATOR

Fortnite and llamas go hand in hand, so the Llaminator harvesting tool has been used by countless players. It can be found in the Lloose Cannon set and is the trademark tool of Lt. John Llama. This legendary outfit was inspired by a Fortnite fan's drawing and then created for the game! In its own words, never send an alpaca to do a llama's job!

THE HARVESTERS

GUM BRAWLER

It isn't often a harvester brings a dimension of taste to your play, but the Gum Brawler seems to do just that. It is available in its default colour, a bitter variant and a sour variant, and is part of the Chew It Yourself set that belongs to Gumbo. Gumbo's colour schem might look amazing in battle, but they don't half stand out – so don't expect to be stealthy.

DRIP AXE

As part of the Blue Crew set, the Drip Axe has a futuristic vibe that wouldn't look out of place in a spaceship. It looks so slick if you use the Professor Slurpo outfit and the Slurp Jet back bling! The great thing about the Drip Axe is that it is powered by Slurp Juice, and it drips slurp every time you use it. That may sound messy, but you don't have to clean it up!

MACE OF HEARTS

This unique harvesting tool is only attainable by playing 30 minutes in a certain Fortnite Creative Mode map. Synthrace Qualifier Creative Mayhem 2 is a futuristic racing map involving a winding circuit, fast cars and epic assault course elements. Complete 30 minutes and the Mace of Hearts was your reward - although it isn't always available. So act fast if it is!

MEGAVOLT

As its name suggests, there is a real electric charge within this harvesting tool. That might not help you harvest any quicker, but it will look absolutely incredible. It is part of the Wild Shock set, along with the outfit Hotwire. Any opponents that witness their mysterious electrical theme will be left in ... a state of shock! Its voltage might not be felt, but it is mega!

NUZZLE JET

Show some love with the Nuzzle Jet harvesting tool. Featuring genuine hug-blasted mecha-strike action, this was one of several accessories only available to Fortnite Crew members for a limited amount of time. It came with the Mecha Cuddle Master outfit, which might sound nice and snuggly – but it was a sinister outfit that wanted to spread fear by cuddling!

STAR WAND

Swing for the stars with this harvesting tool that really allows you to show off your star power! The Star Wand might not look like the scariest accessory you can wield on the island, but let's be honest – sometimes you just want to have fun and swing with a smile on your face. Just be warned: you might be smiling, but the Star Wand stands out like a sore thumb – so expect to attract unwanted attention.

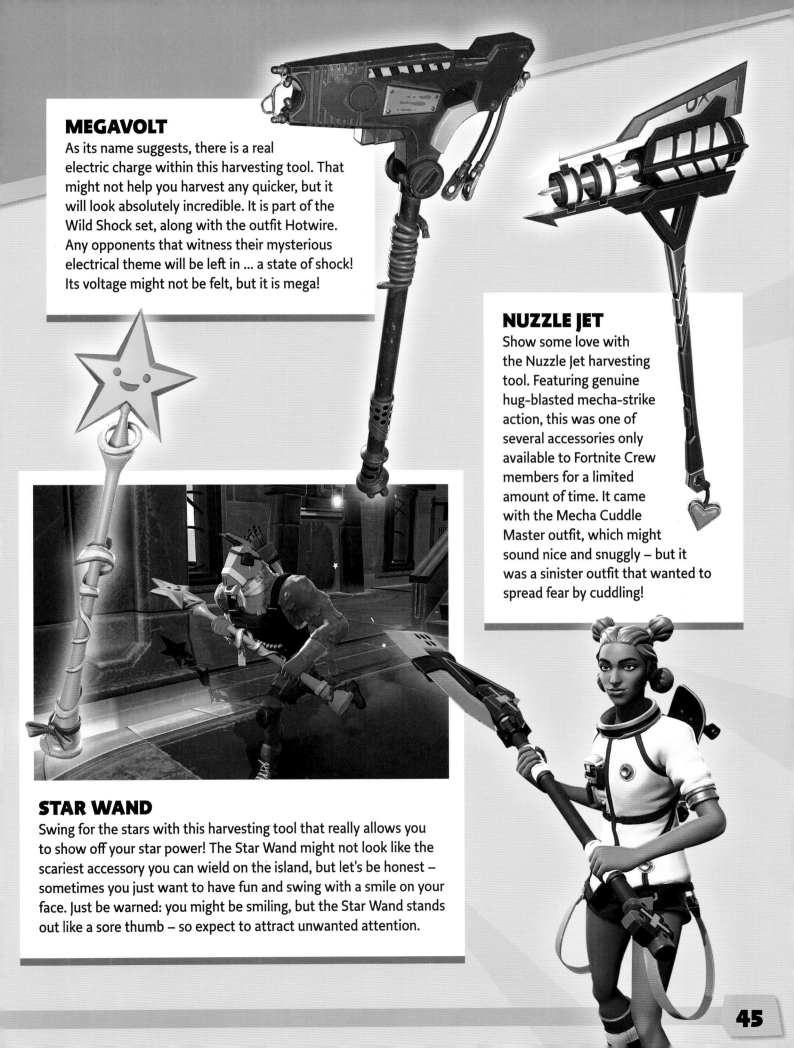

45

GETTING CREATIVE 2

RACE AGAINST WATER 1401-7257-0487

This is kind of 'Floor is Lava' but with water instead of the hot stuff! All you need to do is race through an obstacle course and beat your friends to the top. However, there is some super dangerous water that will slowly rise and swallow the course. If you touch that water, you will take damage.

This race becomes utter chaos as you all scramble to leap over gaps and cling on to the smallest ledges, without dropping into the water. The last thing you want is to get stuck down there or it's elimination for you. All while your friends dance at the finish line.

BOUNTY HUNTER GUN GAME 6343-4288-5725

You may have already played a form of Gun Game elsewhere. It's a popular battle mode that tests your skills with lots of different weapons. You're dropped into an arena and the only goal is to score 15 points in order to win. To do this, you're given a weapon to eliminate other players. The trick is, once you score an elimination, your gun is swapped for another.

This keeps happening until someone wins the game. It's a huge test of how good you are with different weapons. Maybe you're a crackshot with a Ranger Assault Rifle, but not so good with shotguns? There are several rounds to play, so keep fighting and see if your skills get you to the top spot.

ONE ROOM ESCAPE 0300-9657-7369

This escape room is very tricky. Whether you play on your own or with friends, the tasks you need to complete to escape will have you scratching your head. There are puzzles and riddles, as well as some really tough parkour.

The aim is to flick a number of switches which unlock a chest. Opening this chest allows you to progress further, or even to escape completely. You'll need to bring your movement skills, but also a pad and pen to help work out the answers to some puzzles. You can't shoot your way out, and you also can't sprint or mantle the ledges. This is an old school puzzle game.

200 LEVEL PARKOUR RUN 9343-5124-9372

If parkour is your thing, then this collection of death run obstacles is a must-play!

You have 200 levels to beat and, while they start off rather easy, they soon become devilishly difficult. You'll have to make small hopping jumps, huge sprints and leap through gaps, plus dodging lots of spike traps.

There is no easy way to the end, but you can respawn as often as you like. It's not a case of will you fail but how many times will you fail? Get ready for the biggest challenge of your Fortnite career!

THE GLIDERS

Jumping out of the Battle Bus and freefalling down onto the island is the best way to start a Battle Royale match. Your choice of glider won't give you any aero advantages – but it will help you creat an epic look!

BOMBS AWAY

Fortnite players had always held on to the bottom of their gliders, but this epic item changed the game. Designed for players to ride on top of, Bombs Away gives you the ability to sky surf down to your chosen dropzone. Don't be concerned by the name – it doesn't explode when you land!

CORAL CRUISER

Cruising from the Battle Bus to the island is always more fun if you look a bit bonkers, and the Coral Cruisder glider is the craziest glider in the sky. As part of the famous Fish Food set, it might not be the most menacing look, but it will sureLY confuse and alarm your enemies! The only question remaining is ... how does IT catch any air?

OHM

Owl-right then, what is this weird winged contraption? Who knew that mechanical owls could look so creepy? You should ask the owner of this glider, Jules. As part of the Intrepid Engines set, who knows what mechanical mayhem is going on within its armour. Using this glider is a real hoot!

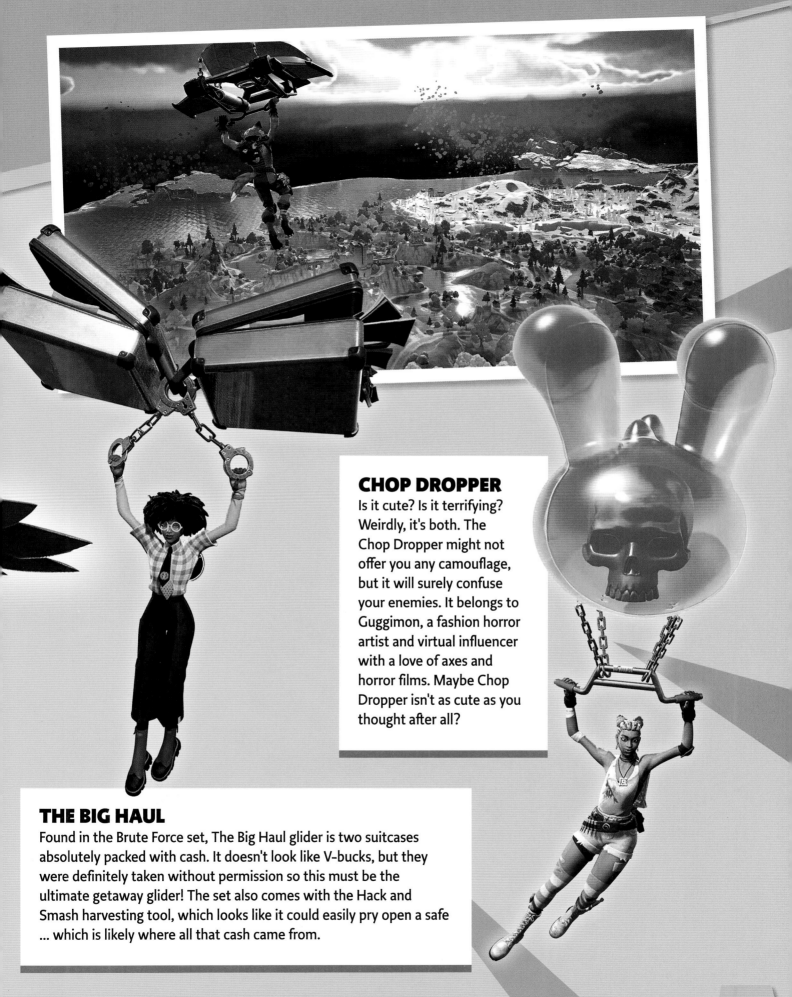

CHOP DROPPER

Is it cute? Is it terrifying? Weirdly, it's both. The Chop Dropper might not offer you any camouflage, but it will surely confuse your enemies. It belongs to Guggimon, a fashion horror artist and virtual influencer with a love of axes and horror films. Maybe Chop Dropper isn't as cute as you thought after all?

THE BIG HAUL

Found in the Brute Force set, The Big Haul glider is two suitcases absolutely packed with cash. It doesn't look like V-bucks, but they were definitely taken without permission so this must be the ultimate getaway glider! The set also comes with the Hack and Smash harvesting tool, which looks like it could easily pry open a safe ... which is likely where all that cash came from.

THE GLIDERS

SKELLEFISH

The catch of the day is here and it's a bit boney. You can positively soar through the sky with this fishy glider, which may have a cute face but it is definitely a little bit on the undead side. That doesn't mean it isn't one of Meowsicles' preferred gliders, though. That feline fighter just loves being reminded of its favourite food!

FORTILLA FLIER

If you achieved Victory in any match during Chapter 2, Season 3, you were rewarded with this glider. It might have SOS painted along the top but you won't need any help when using this to glide down to your chosen drop zone. It looks like it was thrown together with junk but other players will know how you got it and realise they should fear you.

THE ROCKET WING

Dropping into the action has never been as super-charged as with The Rocket Wing. You could only get this glider by completing The Foundation Quests, and it came with The Foundation outfit to wear too. The Rocket Wing looks extra fast and lets you soar into action.

PTERODACTYL

The Pterodactyl takes gliding back to the age of the dinosaurs, with its ferocious beak and deadly talons. Hang on one second, something doesn't seem right. This cretaceous creature looks like it is pieced together by spare mechanical parts. Oh well, if it glides then its worth having a ride on and, on the plus side, it won't try to eat you!

OLLIE

It may not look aerodynamic, but Ollie can float as well as any glider in this list. Those feathers sure do make for a smooth flight, but be ready for a bumpy landing as everyone will see you coming!

WOOLY MAMMOTH

This over the top monster truck is a beast of a glider. With its roaring engine and huge tyres, it will ram anyone out of its way to land safely in your chosen drop zone. Just hope you don't get a flat tyre, because that will seriously reduce your amount of air time! You might have guessed from its ear details that this is the property of Lt. John Llama!

THE BACK BLING

Back blings are a great way to express yourself, and so many of them match up with different skins. The backpacks aren't often sold on their own, they tend to come paired up with a skin or as part of a set. Back blings can be simple backpacks or moving creatures – which style is your favourite?

SIX STRING

Totally tuned-in for mayhem, this squealing back bling is the loudest of them all. It certainly strikes a chord with rockers that want to roll over their enemies with ease. Just keep it down if you're trying to hide later in the game!

GUMMY SACK

Nothing fits better into the Chew It Yourself set than the Gummy Sack. So tasty! But be warned, you need to be cautious of enemies being able to follow your sweet scent. Any with a sweet tooth will track you down in no time at all.

ADVENTURE PACK

If you're looking to survive as long as possible and enjoy an epic adventure, then this is the back bling for you. You'll look the part as you explore every inch of the island in a quest for the greatest loot that will take you into the top 10!

BANANA BRIEFCASE

No one is sure why this smart briefcase is stuffed with oversized bananas, but surely Peely was involved? The bright yellow colour makes it hard to blend into any environments, so always use this wicked bling carefully.

UNICORN FLAKES

It is said that breakfast is the most important meal of the day, and preparation is key when you're heading to the Fortnite island. These sugar-coated treats will keep you full of energy to take on the toughest of foes.

KABAG!

Anything good enough for Midas is good enough for us. This fashionably explosive bling will look great on whatever skin you play in and can be upgraded to a gold version. Perfect for showing off your supreme island skills.

BLISTER PACK

Action figures don't come more action-packed than this Blister Pack. As part of the Agent Jonesy set, it features the Fortnite legend Jonesy in mini, martial arts format. Don't let it get damaged as it could be worth something one day.

FRACTURED WORLD

Don't panic ... the world exploding on your back can't be a bad thing. It could be a terrible thing, though! This epic back bling is part of the space-themed Galaxia set, which also came with the epic Cosmic Llamacorn harvesting tool.

THE BATTLE PASS

The Battle Pass is a huge part of the game and allows you to unlock loads of exclusive skins and items. Anything that comes with the Battle Pass will never be available in the shop, so if you like to collect exclusive skins, this is the only way to get a few for your collection. Here are a few tips to help you get the most from the pass.

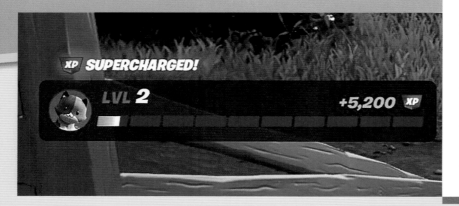

XP BOOST

Don't worry too much if you miss a few days playing and levelling-up your Battle Pass. When you next sign in to play, you'll have an XP boost applied to your account. This means everything you do will earn you more XP and you'll catch-up quickly. It will feel great to see all those stars unlock after a week of not playing!

DAMAGING AND ELIMINATING OPPONENTS

There will always be challenges for damaging or eliminating your opponents. If your combat skills aren't as high as you'd like, working with someone else can really help. For example, if you need to eliminate players, you can ask your teammate to help damage them, leaving the last couple of shots for you. Remember, when the blue numbers stop, the enemy is out of shield and it won't be long before they're goners.

WORK WITH A GROUP

Following on from the last tip, you will always do better when playing with your friends. You can share tips and tricks for beating challenges, or support each other in-game. For example, you might have a challenge to perform tricks on a dirt bike, so find a great spot for it and have your friends watch for enemies while you land your tricks. Then switch roles. You can also carry gas cans for long journeys between POIs or carry healing items for each other to help survive fight challenges.

LEARN THE MAP

If you want to smash through your challenges, a great place to start is to learn the map. Check out every POI and all the little landmarks in between. This map knowledge will be important when a Battle Pass challenge means you must travel between POIs or drop down to certain spots. This will also help you when battling other players, too. If you know a few POIs really well, you can move around the buildings tactically.

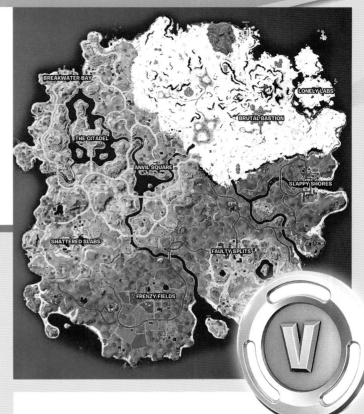

CHECK IT OUT BEFORE BUYING IT

As soon as a new Battle Pass drops with a new season, check it out page-by-page first. Find the skins and items you like and plan to work towards them. The pass earns you stars and you can choose to spend those stars whenever you choose. It's worth remembering, often you have to complete pages to unlock a new skin.

USE THE FREE V-BUCKS TO BUY LEVELS

As you move through the Battle Pass, you'll notice that you can spend stars on V-bucks. Each page features 100 V-bucks to buy. You can do several things with these, like saving them up for the next Battle Pass or to buy skins in the shop. However, you can also buy Battle Pass levels which give you more stars. This is great for the end of the season, if you're falling behind.

GO BEYOND

It's clear that some people play A LOT of Fortnite. Many of you will unlock everything in your Battle Pass after hitting level 100, but it doesn't stop there. The more levels you hit, the more stars you can earn to unlock new variants of the season's skins. Only the grinders and the best players will rock those skins, so get playing to access to the rarest skins!

THE STEPS TO SUCCESS

There are many ways to enjoy Fortnite nowadays, especially with the no-build game mode. There are lots of challenges to complete and places to visit during a match. Whether you love exploring, or simply enjoy winning, here are a whole heap of tips to ensure you have a great time in every battle.

ASSAULT RIFLES ARE JUST AS GOOD AS SNIPERS

When fighting at long range, you don't have to use a sniper or bow. Any assault rifle can reach that far, you just have to steady your aim. While this technique doesn't land as much damage in one shot, you can shoot faster and cause more damage per second. It takes some getting used to, but eventually you'll be landing headshots.

Using an AR rather than a sniper rifle also means you can still see around you, rather than have it blocked-off in the scoped view. This is invaluable if you're trying to remain undetected while you attack.

PLAY WITH FRIENDS

If you're struggling to get a win on your own, try to pull your friends or family into a few games. When playing as a team, you're more likely to get further into the game and reach the later storm circles. You can rely on your team to help eliminate players, or revive you if you get knocked down.

If you choose to play in a team, play smart and learn to share ammo and health drops. Some teams like to keep all their heals on one player, but if they fall in a fight, you will all suffer. Practise quick-dropping your ammo and healing supplies, as this will really help your team!

USE THE VEHICLES

The Fortnite map is big, and it definitely feels that way when you need to get from one side to the other. It can't be said enough, you must use the vehicles! Whether it's a car or a dirt bike, hopping onboard will keep you much safer than running. Dirt bikes are fast enough to speed past other players who may target you, and cars obviously keep you covered constantly.

Cars are always the best option if you're playing as a squad, as they avoid anyone falling behind. Your teammates can also lean out the windows to fire on any incoming enemies, which will help protect the driver.

LEARN CALL OUTS

You can check out common Fortnite language on pages 40-41 and see if there's anything there that you can add to your call outs, but this goes beyond those examples. Call outs are generally used to describe where an item or player can be found. If you play with the same team all the time, you can come up with your own names for locations or buildings within them.

Just basic call outs work though. By saying "two upstairs" your will know two opponents are waiting in the top of a structure. If you call "one going left to right", your squad knows one enemy is running from the left hand side of the screen, to the right. This helps your team target them!

THE STEPS TO SUCCESS

JUMP OR NO JUMP

When it comes down to a one-on-one fight, so many players will jump around while trying to land shotgun hits on you. The main reason why they do this is because it makes them harder to hit, but this isn't always the case. If you use SMGs, you can practise hitting jumping enemies as they move, by either following them with your crosshair as you spray ammo, or by blasting them with a shotgun when they hit the ground.

Whether you decide to jump or not depends on how confident you are landing your shots while you jump. Sometimes, it can be better to take a few shots at your opponent and then start jumping, as they won't expect it.

PROGRAM YOUR HOTBAR

If you dive into your settings, you can scroll across to the little cogwheel symbol, then go to the combat section and find 'Preferred item slots'. In here, you can select what weapons and items you prefer in each of the five loadout slots. So, if you like to have your assault rifle in the first slot, you can choose that. This means that, when collecting loot in a match, it will automatically move the gun or healing item to the spot you like. This cuts down on menu management and keeps you playing and alert. You'll also always know what to select in the heat of a battle.

DON'T BE AFRAID TO RUN AWAY

While it might not feel right at the time, running away is always an option. If you're struggling against an opponent (or they've taken out your team) you can run away to gather your thoughts and reload, before re-engaging the fight. Keeping a vehicle nearby is a big help, as are the throwable launch pads. Just be aware that you're an easy target when you use one to launch!

You don't need to run far, you can quickly move to a nearby structure, take a breath, then get back to the fight. A quick break is all you need to come back stronger.

HOW TO ROTATE

If you watch other people play Fortnite online, you may have heard them talk about rotating. If you're unsure what this means, it can be explained easily. Rotating is the way you move across the map as the storm moves in. Usually, a rotation will be the path you often take to loot along the way.

For example, if you always drop on the south-east edge island, you might always travel up the right-hand side of the map and then towards the middle. This is your rotation path. Knowing when to rotate comes with experience – some people leave it late and take some storm damage, while others will get into zone early and hold the ground. Both can offer benefits and dangers.

THE STEPS TO SUCCESS

HIGH GROUND IS YOUR FRIEND

There's a reason why so many pro players either build up, or search for hills and tall buildings. Having high ground in a fight puts you at an advantage compared to your enemy. The main reason for this is because you'll be able to see further, and spot any enemies before they notice you. This allows you to follow their movement and plan an attack.

If you like to use a sniper or bow, taking the high ground will provide you with the best platform to see further and make the most of your scopes. If you're playing as a team and you're confident in your friends, you can sit on a hill watching over them with a sniper rifle as they explore. This advanced tactic will help keep them safe and gather loot for you both.

USE THE PING SYSTEM

An efficient way to help your team is with the ping system. A lot of people forget to use pings to communicate with teammates. This doesn't only help with your friends, but it's great for when you play in a squad with random people. All you need to do is tap the ping button to show a point on the map – and your team will know where some loot is or where a safe building may be.

If you are targeting with your gun while you ping, it will create a 'danger' icon. This is perfect for if you spot another player or team and need to alert your teammates.

PRACTISE YOUR BUILDING

You might choose to play traditional Fortnite, which includes the old school building. If this is your jam, then you must, must practise building. There are plenty of creative games you can use that help you build faster and swap weapons while placing walls, etc.

If needs be, you can challenge your friends in Battle Labs and see who can build the fastest, or ask them to try and eliminate you while you're placing walls, floors and ramps. The quicker you can build, the more chance you'll have of winning battles because you'll be able to keep a barrier between you and enemies.

MAJOR CHARACTERS

There have been many memorable faces across the history of Fortnite. They've all been involved in epic battles and the stories that have kept you entertained for years. Here is a look at some of the very greatest!

PEELY

Peely has become one of the game's most popular characters since his introduction in Chapter 1, Season 8. They first appeared in the Battle Pass and quickly became a fan favourite. Peely was the first adventure buddy of Jonesy the First, as they teamed up to battle the constant evils. Much like Jonesy, Peely has taken on many forms. In Season 9, they were turned into a smoothie, Season X brought him back to life, and in Chapter 2, Season 2, he became a secret agent. Peely was later accused of vandalising The Foundation statue, and in the next season he formally joined The Seven resistance.

MIDAS

Midas was a major character during the events of Chapter 2. He was a founding member of Shadow and the leader of Ghost. During his time at The Agency, he began building a device which would explode and push the island's storm back. This plan failed, as the storm was too strong and it became a wall of water which flooded the island. Since these events, Midas hasn't been seen. They were a boss to defeat in Season 2, where you could eliminate them and grab their Drum Gun.

THE PARADIGM

Another member of The Seven, she worked with the Imagined Order but everyone thought she was a traitor. It was only after she piloted the Mecha Strike Commander and destroyed The Collider machine, that she was welcomed back to The Seven.

At the end of Chapter 3, The Paradigm watched as the chrome took over the island, thanks to The Herald. Paradigm flew into the Zero Point in order to reset the island for Chapter 4. A heroic action!

THE AGELESS

In Chapter 4, Season 1, an ageless assassin became available. Although it was hard to unlock this skin, the effort was worth it. As part of the Dominion's Dawn set, the blend of medieval fighter and high tech battler is one of the slickest mixes in the game. Fans could get their hands on The Ageless Champion style, if they unlocked all the cosmetics and spent 9 Battle Stars.

MAJOR CHARACTERS

THE FOUNDATION

The Foundation is the leader of The Seven, and his mission is everything. As guardian of the island, it's often up to him and the rest of The Seven to ensure the safety of the land as we know it. He's a heroic character, being kept alive by the suit he wears – a suit which allows him to live across infinite realities. He has been an important part of most of the events we've watched, and played in, across all chapters.

DOCTOR SLONE

Slone was a member of the Imagined Order, and it was her job to try and beat The Seven using her scientific knowledge. Slone had been operating within the island for some time before she captured Jonesy in Season 8 of Chapter 2. As The End event kicked off, we saw her torturing poor Jonesy, before The Foundation saved the day. She was the mastermind behind trying to sabotage the island until she was crushed by the Mecha Strike Commander.

JONESY

Jonesy has appeared in many forms throughout the Fortnite history. As a friend of The Seven, Jonesy has battled against all of the evils who try to take over the island. It's worth remembering that Jonesy the First is the original hero. Over time, Jonesy has taken snapshots of himself when needed for each situation and has become Bunker Jonesy, Recruit Jonesy, Agent Jones and Battalion Brawler. It's a little confusing, so as the man himself says "Jonesy the First, the most important one."

THE CUBE QUEEN

The Cube Queen is one of the most evil enemies the island has seen. She and her army of cubes enter different realities and destroy them from the inside. This helps her rule over any world while they crumble. The Cube Queen was responsible for sending a cube in Chapter 1, which fans named Kevin! That cube failed to wipe out the island, so she came to do it herself throughout Chapter 2. She was defeated when the island was flipped, which plunged her into the ocean and she was never seen again.

THE STORY SO FAR

Chapter 3 of Fortnite may have been the shortest so far, but it was packed with new story information and characters, making big changes to the world we know. The chapter started and ended with a new map and a new direction for the story to follow. Let's take a trip through every main bit of the action.

FLIPPING OUT – SEASON 1

Chapter 3 started out with the island literally being flipped upside down. This was done in order to stop Doctor Slone and the Imagined Order, and their plans to take over the island and control the Zero Point within.

The Looper (that was you!) wakes at Looper Landing, and The Foundation explains that the Imagined Order wanted to use the Zero Point to further their plans. Although the map was flipped, it doesn't mean the threat of the Imagined Order has ended.

The Omniverse (all of Fortnite) is in constant danger. This is discovered quickly, as it seems some of the Imagined Order were left clinging on. They want to get through to the new world, and use driller vehicles to drill through the map from below.

As they break through, the Imagined Order appear in five teams and begin approaching The Sanctuary, which is the home of The Seven. Here, players could listen to a secret broadcast from The Scientist, who is trying to get the help from The Paradigm. It was a clear warning that war was coming to the island, so The Seven plan to launch recon rockets to scout for help.

The Imagined Order sabotage the launch and the ending of Season 1 had The Scientist team up with players across the world to stop the Imagined Order once and for all.

TIME FOR WAR – SEASON 2

The Imagined Order are held back, but not defeated. They plan to unleash war on everyone across the island. A giant drill has emerged from underneath the map, and the Imagined Order begin battling all players.

The map begins to split into zones, some under the control of the Imagined Order and some held by the resistance. Huge tanks and airships are seen across the island. The airships are filled with great loot and Imagined Order troops, while the tanks can be piloted by players to help win the war.

Portals opened across the Omniverse and two new members of The Seven are introduced – The Imagined and The Origin. Jones, The Origin and The Imagined team up with players to counterattack the Imagined Order and gain an advantage. Slowly the Imagined Order's zones start to reduce.

Now, Agent Jones hears that the Imagined Order are building a Doomsday device to destroy everything. They build The Collider to blow up the Zero Point and destroy all players and the island!

In order to prevent the explosion, The Paradigm piloted Mecha Team Leader. The final event of the season saw the giant mech back online and crush Doctor Slone, and her tank with the mocha fist.

The Paradigm raised players, along with Jones and The Foundation, who jump through a Zero Point portal which opened near The Collider but it reveals a new enemy. The players came together to destroy The Collider and Season 2 ends.

THE STORY SO FAR

THE REALITY TREE – SEASON 3

With the Imagined Order defeated and The Collider destroyed, the island begins to party. Paint is splashing everywhere, loud music is blasting and anyone who's anyone is celebrating the win over evil. In its own words, the island is vibin'.

After The Collider explodes, the Zero Point is exposed and it forms The Reality Tree. This tree begins to lay roots throughout the island, sprouting up smaller trees which players could loot for rare and legendary gear.

Large roots break through the ground across the entire island, and slowly everything begins to look and feel very different. The Scientist steps in to test sections of the tree and realises that exposing the Zero Point – and freeing it – was a bad idea.

The Scientist builds an A.I. called A.M.I.E, who works with all players to piece together the mysterious relics that are coming from the main tree. It's thought that these relics were a message from the tree (and the island) warning us that danger is coming ...

The Paradigm asks players to track down The Foundation, who hasn't been seen since jumping through the portal with Agent Jones. Meanwhile, The Scientist, The Visitor and The Origin have been researching a weird substance in their lab. This substance has begun leaking through to the island.

When they find out that The Scientist has left the island, players were left scurrying around in chaos. The Paradigm also goes missing, disappearing to a place unknown, leaving only brave players and A.M.I.E alone on the island with the substance.

CHROME – SEASON 4

The strange substance is discovered to be metallic and has the name Chrome, and it begins to take over the entire island. It oozes into areas, turning everything silver, even the weapons. While this happens, the remaining members of The Seven head out to find the others who are lost away in a different reality.

While all this chaos happens, The Herald appears. She is the cause of the Chrome spreading and has been watching everything closely. She sets up a base on the island and begins turning reality into the Last Reality, a place where she thrives, but nothing else does.

A company called No Sweat Insurance, who oversee the buildings on the island, begin to float important areas above all of the Chrome. They try to save each area, one by one. An old Imagined Order airship is taken over by players as they save islanders.

Soon, The Paradigm gets in touch with Jones to arrange a way to halt The Nothing, which The Herald is bringing. The Loopers begin to investigate the Reality Roots and also find battle plans written by The Origin.

As The Herald's power begins to grow, players built a stronghold within the Reality Tree. The fight was coming and it was hard to know who will survive. Suddenly, huge Chrome Vortex begins to rip at the Reality Tree. The Herald has waited long enough and the war has started.

The Herald continues to grow in size and is totally covered with Chrome. Weapons stop working on her, as she fuses with the Reality Tree. Doing this, she sacrifices herself as she tries to complete the destruction of the island … killing everyone.

Somehow, the Zero Point survives but players are left drifting in space with chunks of the island. The season event requires players to piece together all the chunks of land by finding energy in other small dimensions. The Zero Point begins pulling in the land, slowly piecing it all together to form a brand new island, where Chapter 4 comes to an end. What awaits us next?